11+ Vocabulary, Verbal Reasoning for GL Assessment
© Jane Armstrong, 2020

Published : Jane Armstrong, 2020

Please read the following carefully before you begin the tests.

- Each test should take no more than 10 minutes. It is wise to get into the habit of limiting the time you spend on each test. This is good preparation for the real thing.

- Read the title of the question carefully. Many points have been lost by a child mistaking a request for antonyms rather than synonyms for example.

- Use each question as an opportunity to broaden your vocabulary. Once you have completed a test make a note of any words you may not have heard of before and look them up online or in a dictionary. Also find out if they have an antonym or synonym.

- Good luck and have fun. You will learn more and want to continue learning if you are enjoying yourself.

Test 1

1. Opposite meaning

Find two words, one from each group, that are most opposite in meaning.
Underline the two words as shown in the example.

Example   (milk, <u>divide</u>, angry)   (cross, wine, <u>multiply</u>)

a.   (resist, hold, insist)   (turn, accede, refute)

b.   (drive, top, heed)   (disregard, direct, pay)

c.   (flourish, leaf, stem)   (grow, reproduce, wither)

d.   (neaten, carry, holdall)   (hold, disorganise, steal)

e.   (mine, quarry, excavate)   (dig, bury, hollow)

2. Closest in meaning

Find two words, one from each group, that are closest in meaning.
Underline the two words as shown in the example.

Example   (<u>chaos</u>, affinity, rebuke)   (order, <u>havoc</u>, wipe)

a.   (shrink, expel, omit)   (emit, contract, contain)

b.   (purposeful, strong, thin)   (deliberate, hardy, tall)

c.   (forest, confused, quiet)   (bewildered, firm, knowing)

d.   (rectify, vapour, hurt)   (heal, wind, wound)

3.   Choose a word

Choose the most appropriate word to complete the sentences.

The modern (1) _____ (beam, jump, boom) in early map collecting, as far as it relates to the amateur collector, probably dates back to the 1920's.   Today, map collecting has become so popular that it enjoys a society of its own and a highly popular (2) _____ (diary, journal, citation), which features articles on the history of (3) _____ (entomology, biology, cartography) together with reviews, news articles and auction prices.   In addition to this, numerous regional and local societies are (4) _____ (flowering, flouring, flourishing), particularly in America.   Prices for early maps have (5) _____ (raised, risen, rise) enormously since the 1950's as many collectors look upon them as a form of investment.   Others (6) _____ (bass, base, bias) their collections around a theme: maps from their home country, maps by a certain mapmaker or maps from a certain period in time.

Did you know the word 'map' comes from the Latin phrase 'Mappa mundi'. 'Mappa' meant napkin or cloth and 'mundi' meant the world. Thus 'map' became a shortened version of 'a two-dimensional representation of the surface of the world'.

Test 2

1. Fill in the missing words

Choose the most appropriate word from the list available to complete the following passage. Two of the words will not be needed.

notorious	order	Earl	outside	start	details	sparked

The Yorkshire Rebellion was _____ off by resentment of the taxation granted

by Parliament in 1489 in _____ to finance the involvement of English forces in the

campaign in Brittany, France.   It became particularly _____ because of the

murder, by the rebels, of the Earl of Northumberland just _____ Topcliffe near

Thirsk in the North Riding of Yorkshire in April of that year.   There are not many

_____ surrounding the rebellion but the Earl of Northumberland was considered

to be a victim of resentment against taxation.

2. Closest in meaning

Find two words, one from each group, that are closest in meaning.
Underline the two words as shown in the example.

Example   (<u>chaos</u>, affinity, rebuke)   (order, <u>havoc</u>, wipe)

a.   (assessment, jury, compare)   (purchase, buy, evaluation)

b.   (admit, reject, spoken)   (sanction, decline, decrease)

c.   (petty, major, pertinent)   (task, trivial, ordinary)

d.   (chief, inferior, tactile)   (worse, ordinary, govern)

3. Idioms

Match the idiom in **bold** to its meaning.

A blessing in disguise	a. good luck
Cut someone some slack	b. get out of control
Break a leg	c. a good thing that seemed bad at first
Get out of hand	d. don't give up
Hang in there	e. don't be so critical

4. Opposite meaning

Find two words, one from each group, that are most opposite in meaning.
Underline the two words as shown in the example.

Example   (milk, <u>divide</u>, angry)   (cross, wine, <u>multiply</u>)

a.   (educated, school, boring)   (informed, ignorant, replete)

b.   (famous, idolised, verb)   (acclaimed, unknown, noun)

c.   (peculiar, plural, strange)   (singular, eminent, binary)

d.   (entity, deed, reality)   (substance, fantasy, matter)

e.   (inaudible, whisper, utter)   (spoken, fast, loud)

Did you know the word 'audible' comes from the Latin word 'audire' meaning 'to hear'. The loudest sound ever recorded occurred when the volcano Krakatoa exploded in 1883, it registered over 170 decibels and could be heard over 3000 miles away.

Test 3

1. Opposite meaning

Find two words, one from each group, that are most opposite in meaning.
Underline the two words as shown in the example.

Example   (milk, <u>divide</u>, angry)   (cross, wine, <u>multiply</u>)

a.   (spread, seed, scarce)   (sparse, plentiful, heavy)

b.   (awake, hazy, vague)   (amorphous, loose, precise)

c.   (append, carry, include)   (insert, omit, emit)

d.   (supporter, ally, patron)   (player, traitor, top)

e.   (edgy, perilous, fall)   (weak, week, safe)

2. Fill in the missing words

Choose the most appropriate word from the list available to complete the following passage.
Two of the words will not be needed.

ensuing	extending	introduced	dining	later	long	century

The use of sliding parts in furniture gave us the _____ or draw leaf dining table.

First _____ during the late sixteenth _____, this type of table

became popular in the Jacobean period. Variations of the draw leaf construction were

produced throughout the _____ periods to the present day, and many of our

modern extending tables work on the same basic principle as the Elizabethan version. When

closed, the table looks like a long _____ table with legs.

3. Word Groups

Look at these groups of words.

A	B	C	D
cold	grape	ash	trout
sneeze	apple	hazel	cod

Now choose the corresponding group for each of the following words. Write the letter in the space provided.

salmon _____   elm _____   oak _____   flu _____   orange _____

eel _____   fever _____   beech _____   lemon _____   plaice _____

Plaice can grow up to 60cm long and are a wide, flat fish. The word 'plaice' comes from the Old French word 'plaiz', which in turn derived from the Latin word 'platessa', which itself came from the Greek word 'platus' meaning 'broad'.

Test 4

1. Opposite meaning

Find two words, one from each group, that are most opposite in meaning.
Underline the two words as shown in the example.

Example   (milk, <u>divide</u>, angry)   (cross, wine, <u>multiply</u>)

a.   (reuse, increase, recycle)   (plenty, spread, reduce)

b.   (calm, handle, stretch)   (soothe, turbulent, stroke)

c.   (elementary, placid, multiply)   (simple, complicated, dry)

d.   (generous, gregarious, portion)   (quiet, piece, miserly)

e.   (elongate, halt, proceed)   (continue, maintain, finish)

2. Insert a letter

Write in the missing letter that will finish the first word and start the second.

Example   oxe (**n**) ail

bor (   ) ast   boo (   ) nee   gro (   ) ish   tea (   ) ick

crow (   ) od   pon (   ) uck   sit (   ) ver   pos (   ) uck

3.   Idioms

Match the idiom in **bold** to its meaning.

Miss the boat		a. To stop doing something
To get bent out of shape		b. It's too late
Call it a day		c. To be treated as you treat others (usually badly)
By the skin of your teeth		d. To get upset about something
Get a taste of your own medicine		e. Just barely

The origin of the phrase 'Get a taste of your own medicine' comes from a famous story by Aesop about a swindler who sells fake medicine. When he falls ill, people give him his own medicine, which they know will not work to make him better.

Test 5

1. Opposite meaning

Find two words, one from each group, that are most opposite in meaning.
Underline the two words as shown in the example.

Example   (milk, <u>divide</u>, angry)   (cross, wine, <u>multiply</u>)

a.   (dry, fruitful, juicy)   (vegetable, futile, tasty)

b.   (hard, smooth, inflexible)   (coiled, bendy, flat)

c.   (midday, dusk, day)   (dawn, light, dark)

d.   (special, different, awkward)   (chaotic, dull, ordinary)

e.   (docile, awake, lazy)   (standing, energetic, upright)

2. Hidden words

Can you find a four letter word hidden in each of the following sentences. The word will consist of a letter or letters from the end of one word and a letter or letters from the start of the next word. Write the word in the space provided.

Example   I used yours after mine ran out.   **term** (after **m**ine)

a.   He replied to her in French.   _____

b   I unstick stamps from envelopes.   _____

c.   The window had four openings at the top.   _____

d.   My hip operation went well.   _____

e.   She collected raw carrots at the allotment.   _____

3.   Alphabetical order

If the letters in the following words are arranged in alphabetical order, which letter would come in the middle?

Example   ADVANCE   _D_

FLOWERS   _____

PROTEIN   _____

HIGHEST   _____

WEBSITE   _____

4.   Insert two letters

Find the two letters that finish the first word and start the second word.

Example   chur   (**ch**)   ain

a.   reme   (   )   ed

b.   fin   (   )   ways

c.   jew   (   )   bow

d.   bro   (   )   vert

e.   glan   (   )   ase

*Did you know, after water, protein is the most abundent substance in the body.
In fact your muscles, organs and immune system are mainly made of protein.*

Test 6

1. Number series

Find the number that continues the sequence in the most sensible way.

Example   2, 4, 6, 8, _ 10 _

a.   16, 16, 17, 19, 22, _____

b.   25, 29, 33, 37, 41, _____

c.   1, 4, 9, 16, 25, 36, _____

d.   93, 85, 78, 72, 67, _____

2. Missing word

Find the three letter word that is missing from the capitalised letters to form a new word.
Write the three letter word and the complete new word as shown in the example.

Example   Tom will GLY do it for you.   **LAD**, GLADLY

a.   George was trying to grow his BD.   _____

b.   They estimated that the JNEY would take two hours.   _____

c.   Mary liked to add RAIS to her cake.   _____

d.   Everyone SD as the bride walked down the aisle.   _____

e.   Eric had the nails ready but could not find his MER.   _____

3. Move a letter

Move one letter from the first word over to the second word to create two new words.

Example   crease   filly   <u>cease</u>   <u>frilly</u>

a.   waiter   bran   _____   _____

b.   driven   raft   _____   _____

c.   fiend   pan   _____   _____

d.   clean   cap   _____   _____

e.   flame   alter   _____   _____

4. Opposite meaning

Find two words, one from each group, that are most opposite in meaning.
Underline the two words as shown in the example.

Example   (milk, <u>divide</u>, angry)   (cross, wine, <u>multiply</u>)

a.   (friend, alley, acquaintance)   (partner, equal, foe)

b.   (smooth, tranquil, waves)   (mixed, agitated, emulsion)

c.   (respectful, rude, impolite)   (evil, impudent, sad)

d.   (continue, commence, bail)   (travel, abandon, start)

Test 7

1. **Alphabetical order**

a. Write the letters of the word COMPLAIN
    in alphabetical order.   _____

b. If the letters in DISTANT are written alphabetically
    which letter comes in the middle?   _____

c. Write the following words in alphabetical order.

FIGHT   FLIGHT   FLOAT   FLAT   FAINT

_____   _____   _____   _____   _____

2. **Compound words**

Can you find a word that can be put after each of the following words to create a new compound word.

Example   door   rail   alley   passage   **way**

a.   snow   fire   fore   show   _____

b.   green   horse   saw   hover   _____

c.   fly   sky   draw   foot   _____

d.   silver   shell   jelly   gold   _____

3. Closest in meaning

Find two words, one from each group, that are closest in meaning.
Underline the two words as shown in the example.

Example   (<u>chaos</u>, affinity, rebuke)   (order, <u>havoc</u>, wipe)

a.   (luminous, clever, vague)   (authority, bright, dim)

b.   (remain, lay, slowly)   (hang, leave, linger)

c.   (nibble, chew, peckish)   (hungry, swallow, thirsty)

d.   (stack, burrow, dig)   (jump, fall, heap)

e.   (emit, elude, loud)   (avoid, omit, allude)

Did you know the word 'chaos' comes from the Greek word 'khaos' meaning 'a void or abyss'.

Test 8

1. Change one word

The following sentences do not make sense. Can you spot the incorrect word? Underline the word that is wrong in each sentence and write the correct word.

Example   Daisy had to <u>undo</u> her seatbelt before her father could start the car. **fasten**

a.   Tom loved to cycle to school as it kept him lazy.   _____

b.   Mum shut the door to see who was there.   _____

c.   Oliver always drinks water when he's hungry.   _____

d.   The question was so easy no one knew the answer.   _____

2. Fill in the missing words

Choose the most appropriate word from the list available to complete the following passage. Two of the words will not be needed.

deed	byelaw	common	act	illegal	liable	present

There is no _____ of Parliament forbidding the pasturing of bulls in fields crossed

by public paths, but most counties have a _____ which makes it illegal to have a

bull more than twelve months old in a field containing a public path. Some counties allow

bulls in fields with paths provided that cows are _____, on the grounds that the

bull will be more interested in the cows than in walkers. It is _____ to have any

animal known to be dangerous in a field crossed by a public path and the owner is

_____ for any damage or injury that the beast may cause.

3. Two odd ones out

Three of the words in the list are linked in some way. Mark the words that are not linked as shown in the example.

Example	walk	~~cook~~	cycle	~~bake~~	hike

a.	banana	parsnip	carrot	apple	turnip
b.	glass	ocean	lake	water	pond
c.	cherish	love	detest	adore	abhor
d.	fox	lion	frog	jaguar	cheetah
e.	subside	ascend	rise	descend	mount

Did you know the highest mountain in Scotland is Ben Nevis at 1345m, the highest in England is Scafell Pike at 978m, the highest in Wales is Snowdon at 1085m and the highest in Ireland is Carrauntoohil at 1039m.

Have you climbed any of them?

Test 9

1.   Number series

Find the missing number from the sequence.

Example   2, 4, 6, 8, __10__

a.   2, 4, 5, 10, 11, 22, _____

b.   85, 84, 80, _____, 63, 50, 34

c.   _____, 16, 17, 14, 15, 12, 13

d.   76, 83, 77, 82, 78, 81, _____

2.   Closest in meaning

Find two words, one from each group, that are closest in meaning.
Underline the two words as shown in the example.

Example   (chaos, affinity, rebuke)   (order, havoc, wipe)

a.   (turbulent, gentle, lively)   (fast, liable, tempestuous)

b.   (fire, cremate, quench)   (incinerate, remove, wet)

c.   (bottomless, flawless, flat)   (perfect, ceiling, faulty)

d.   (extricate, hide, borrow)   (elongate, release, dry)

e.   (soak, dry, damp)   (moist, tepid, hard)

3. Alphabetical order

SPLOTCH   SPECKLE   SPINAL   SPIRIT   SPEARED

If these words were placed in alphabetical order which one would come:

a.   last   _____

b.   first   _____

c.   second   _____

d.   fourth   _____

Did you know the human spine is divided into five sections called 'regions'. They are called the Cervical, Thoracic, Lumbar, Sacral and Coccygeal regions. Each region is made up of vertebrae and there are a total of 33 vertebrae in a human spine.

Test 10

1. Compound words

Can you find a word that can be put after each of the following words to create a new compound word.

Example   door   rail   alley   passage   **way**

a.   which   how   when   whom   _____

b.   spoils   air   pass   sea   _____

c.   court   farm   dock   junk   _____

d.   finger   thumb   blue   news   _____

2. Fill in the missing words

Choose the most appropriate word from the list available to complete the following passage. Two of the words will not be needed.

centre	flat	crust	molten	masses	chemical	pressure

Minerals are _____ substances that occur naturally in the _____ of the earth. Rocks are _____ of one or more minerals. Three great classes of rocks are distinguished: igneous (those that solidified from the _____ state); sedimentary (those formed as a result of the erosion of pre-existing rocks and the redeposition of the resulting material); and metamorphic (rocks formed by the effects of _____ and/or heat on existing rocks).

23

3.   Insert two letters

Find the two letters that finish the first word and start the second word.

Example   chur   (**ch**)   ain

a.   almo   (   )   one

b.   cri   (   )   ge

c.   spin   (   )   mond

d.   dan   (   )   ase

e.   mosa   (   )   icle

Dry ice is the solid form of carbon dioxide. Water usually freezes to become ice at 0°C
but dry ice can reach temperatures as low as -78.5°C.

Test 11

1. Letter series

A B C D E F G H I J K L M N O P Q R S T U V W X Y Z

The alphabet is written above to help you. Find the missing pair of letters in the following sequences. Write the pair of letters in the space provided.

a.　　AH　　BI　　CJ　　DK　　_____

b.　　ZA　　YB　　XC　　WD　　_____

c.　　AB　　EF　　IJ　　OP　　_____

d.　　GE　　HI　　JH　　KL　　_____

2. Opposite meaning

Find two words, one from each group, that are most opposite in meaning.
Underline the two words as shown in the example.

Example　　　(milk, <u>divide</u>, angry)　　　　　　　(cross, wine, <u>multiply</u>)

a.　　　　(napkin, towel, smile)　　　　　　　(frown, black, blue)

b.　　　　(heart, active, inhale)　　　　　　　(breathe, lungs, docile)

c.　　　　(ally, soldier, captain)　　　　　　　(ship, foe, train)

d.　　　　(base, shop, supermarket)　　　　　　(wood, metal, apex)

e.　　　　(nadir, baffle, level)　　　　　　　(top, floor, drop)

3.   Missing word

Find the three letter word that is missing from the capitalised letters to form a new word. Write the three letter word and the complete new word as shown in the example.

Example   Tom will GLY do it for you.   <u>**LAD**, GLADLY</u>

a.   Michael, Emma and Jack GATED by the swings.   _____

b.   I find that totally BEVABLE!   _____

c.   How many people are there in your HOUSEH?   _____

d.   Peter and Sally always hung up MISTOE at Christmas.   _____

e.   The puzzle pieces didn't fit because they were INCONGNT._____

Test 12

1. Move a letter

Move one letter from the first word over to the second word to create two new words.

Example   crease   filly   <u>cease</u>   <u>frilly</u>

a.   beacon   vent   _____   _____

b.   string   camp   _____   _____

c.   movies   host   _____   _____

d.   pitch   hath   _____   _____

2. Fill in the missing words

Choose the most appropriate word from the list available to complete the following passage. Two of the words will not be needed.

investigate	estuary	found	water	Kent	foothills	stage

The Thames rises in the _____ of the Cotswolds and flows eastwards towards Oxford, searching it seems for a gap in the chalk hills to the south. At Oxford it turns south having _____ the gap between the Berkshire Downs and the Chilterns. At this _____ it has grown so wide it appears almost to fill the gap and to leave no room for those twin villages of Streatley and Goring. At Reading, with the help of the river Kennet, it decides to _____ the slopes of the Chilterns. At Marlow the river becomes bored with the chalk and flows southeast through Eton and Windsor, but at Weybridge it is the sea that urges it to flow eastward again through London, and on to lose itself beyond the _____.

3. Change one word

The following sentences do not make sense. Can you spot the incorrect word? Underline the word that is wrong in each sentence and write the correct word.

Example   Daisy had to <u>undo</u> her seatbelt before her father could start the car. **<u>fasten</u>**

a.   Esther was thrilled that she had lost the race.   _____

b.   He sounded different with a moustache.   _____

c.   As the door closed, she realised she'd forgotten her lock.   _____

d.   Tim awoke and decided yesterday would be a good day.   _____

Did you know Albert Einstein had a moustache for over 50 years. And in a standard deck of cards the King of Hearts is the only king without a moustache!

Test 13

1. Insert a letter

Find the letter that finishes the first word and starts the second word.

Example　　　　pon　(**d**)　ash

a.　　thin　(　　　)　naw

b.　　bat　(　　　)　ate

c.　　cloth　(　　　)　aten

d.　　hair　(　　　)　acht

e.　　line　(　　　)　eat

2. Word Groups

Look at these groups of words.

A	B	C	D
fear	red	crab	roof
anger	purple	prawn	wall

Now choose the corresponding group for each of the following words. Write the letter in the space provided.

happiness _____　　window _____　　lobster _____　　floor _____　　taupe _____

shrimp _____　　sorrow _____　　ceiling _____　　regret _____　　lilac _____

29

3.   Hidden words

Can you find a four letter word hidden in each of the following sentences. The word will consist of a letter or letters from the end of one word and a letter or letters from the start of the next word.

Example   I used yours after mine ran out.   **term** (af**ter m**ine)

a.   People who work at sea mostly stay away from home.   _____

b   I can undo ordinary mistakes but this is beyond me.   _____

c.   Our village needs two new youth centres.   _____

d.   Mike and Amelia were always late home.   _____

e.   I couldn't have made it more apparent if I'd tried.   _____

Test 14

1. Word swaps

Find and underline the two words in each of the following sentences that need to swap places for the sentences to make sense. Underline both words.

a.   David wrote a long post before putting it in the envelope ready to letter.

b.   Susan new her wore hat.

c.   Peter took evening lessons on Tuesday swimming.

d.   Always look to remember before crossing the road.

e.   I hope I well do will this afternoon.

2. Opposite meaning

Find two words, one from each group, that are most opposite in meaning.
Underline the two words as shown in the example.

Example   (milk, <u>divide</u>, angry)   (cross, wine, <u>multiply</u>)

a.   (building, destroy, builder)   (build, remove, design)

b.   (perfect, monitor, prefect)   (faulty, screen, keyboard)

c.   (magazine, wallet, comic)   (tragic, book, folder)

d.   (artificial, cheap, plastic)   (genuine, deer, realistic)

e.   (luck, unlucky, wish)   (fortunate, charm, keepsake)

3.   Move a letter

Move one letter from the first word over to the second word to create two new words.

Example   crease   filly   <u>cease</u>   <u>frilly</u>

a.   badger   fog   _____   _____

b.   seal   edge   _____   _____

c.   trap   font   _____   _____

d.   push   bat   _____   _____

e.   rash   bun   _____   _____

Did you know the name for a badger's home is a sett. Some setts can be over 100 years old
as generations of badgers return to the same sett time and time again.

Test 15

1. Number series

Complete the missing numbers in the following sequences.

Example	2	4	6	8	<u>10</u>	<u>12</u>
a.	2	4	8	16	32	___	___
b.	5	10	16	23	___	40	___
c.	3	7	5	___	7	11	___
d.	2	5	___	___	20	27	35
e.	___	55	64	73	___	91	100

2. Letter series

Complete the missing pairs of letters in the following sequences. The alphabet has been given as an aid.

A B C D E F G H I J K L M N O P Q R S T U V W X Y Z

Example	FS	IQ	HO	**KM**	JK	**MI**
a.	LO	MJ	NQ	___	PS	___
b.	YD	XE	WF	VG	___	___
c.	___	UF	XC	SH	VE	___
d.	GP	IQ	KP	___	OP	___

33

3.   Related words

A B C D E F G H I J K L M N O P Q R S T U V W X Y Z

The alphabet is shown above to help you.

a.   If the code for SMALL is UOCNN,
            what is the code for TINY?   _____

b.   If the code for RINSE is SHORF,
            what is the code for TUMBLE?   _____

c.   If the code for DIAMOND is EKDQTTK,
            what is the code for JEWEL?   _____

d.   If the code for DEBIT is ZIXMP,
            what is the code for BALANCE?   _____

Did you know that the world's largest diamond crystal is called the Cullinan diamond. It was discovered in 1905 in a diamond mine in South Africa by a gentleman called Frederick Wells and it weighed a whopping 3106.75 carats.

Test 16

1. Related numbers

Look at the relationship between the first and last number in each set of brackets and use that relationship to find the missing number.

Example   (16 [4] 4)   (15 [3] 5)   (12 [**4**] 3)

a.   (34 [50] 16)   (43 [52] 9)   (21 [**?**] 45)

b.   (72 [13] 59)   (15 [4] 11)   (87 [**?**] 16)

c.   (1 [4] 4)   (2 [10] 5)   (9 [**?**] 2)

d.   (72 [8] 9)   (80 [16] 5)   (21 [**?**] 7)

2. Alphabetical order

If the following words were placed in alphabetical order, which word would come third? Underline the word in each line.

a.	build	beguile	boulder	block	bungee
b.	crane	cricket	crumble	crispy	crush
c.	water	wade	window	wish	wash
d.	forgive	field	feign	foreign	forget

35

3. Letters for numbers

A = 5   B = 7   C = 12 D = 2   E = 3

What are the answers to the following sums? Write your answer as a letter.

a.   A + E = _____ + 1

b.   C ÷ E = B - _____

c.   C x A = 20 x _____

d.   A + C - B = D x _____

Did you know algebra is a branch of mathematics that uses letters to replace numbers where the value of those numbers is unknown. When a calculation in algebra contains an 'equals' sign it is called an equation. The word 'algebra' comes from the arabic word 'al-jabr' which means 'the reunion of broken parts'.

Test 17

1. Opposite meaning

Find two words, one from each group, that are most opposite in meaning.
Underline the two words as shown in the example.

Example	(milk, <u>divide</u>, angry)	(cross, wine, <u>multiply</u>)
a.	(calm, uppity, pompous)	(humble, grandiose, sad)
b.	(radical, liberal, obsolete)	(conservative, typical, free)
c.	(similar, motley, canine)	(drab, coloured, uniform)
d.	(bake, roast, raw)	(grill, cook, cooked)

2. Two odd ones out

Three of the words in the lists below are linked in some way. Mark the words that are not
linked as shown in the example :

Example :	dove	crow	~~cat~~	magpie	~~dog~~
a.	femur	ulna	radius	bicep	deltoid
b.	circle	square	triangle	rhombus	trapezoid
c.	paper	blackboard	pen	whiteboard	pencil
d.	beef	pork	pig	cow	venison
e.	France	Germany	Mexico	Texas	Spain

3.   Missing words

Choose the best word to complete the sentences.

Every watermill (1.) _____ (is, of, has) its own individual characteristics that make it unique.   The arrangement of the watercourses (2.) _____ (whose, then, that) power the wheel will depend upon the mill's location.   Some mills have bypass sluices that appear to plunge the water (3.) _____ (under, into, over) a hole in the ground without any obvious outlet. A few mills have these underground aqueducts that emerge many metres below the mill, usually underneath (4.) _____(an, a, the) overgrown bank that discourages their discovery.   Derelict sites can pose considerable problems to the investigator (5.) _____(whom, whose, who) is seeking to reconstruct the layout.

Test 18

1. Complete the sum

For each question find the missing number that will complete the sum and write it in the space provided.

a. $45 \div 9 = 20 \div$ _____

b. $9 \times 3 - 7 = 10 \times$ _____

c. $54 + 26 = 6 + 2 \times$ _____

d. $19 \times 10 = 80 + 30 +$ _____

2. Closest in meaning

Find two words, one from each group, that are closest in meaning.
Underline the two words as shown in the example.

Example   (<u>chaos</u>, affinity, rebuke)   (order, <u>havoc</u>, wipe)

a.   (wrong, evil, ingenious)   (helpful, good, wicked)

b.   (broad, thin, deep)   (big, small, wide)

c.   (wimpy, anxious, terrified)   (scared, horrified, nervous)

d.   (harsh, pretty, strange)   (pleasant, cruel, angry)

e.   (half, brief, near)   (short, soon, over)

3. Two odd ones out

Three of the words in the list are linked in some way. Draw a line through the words that are not linked, as shown in the example :

Example :   dove   crow   ~~eat~~   magpie   ~~dog~~

a.   red   green   flag   pole   blue

b.   guitar   music   volume   violin   cello

c.   see   hear   sound   smell   nose

d.   snow   sleet   sun   rain   rays

e.   shirt   trilby   moccasins   bowler   cap

Did you know that the bowler hat was originally invented in 1849 for the British politician and soldier Edward Coke. They were popular amongst the working classes in Britain during the Victorian era and also in the American West where they were worn more often than a cowboy hat or sombrero.

Test 19

1. Fill in the missing words

Choose the most appropriate word from the list available to complete the following passage. One of the words will not be needed.

active	country	the	compute	part	those	tall

The spirit of cycling is very much alive in most of _____ countries of the world,

and it looks as though it will continue that way for a long time to come, certainly as long as

there are _____ people wishing to travel about in the most convenient and

inexpensive way imaginable. It would be almost impossible to _____ the number

of bicycles in existence—certainly several millions in this _____ alone, and this

represents a major industry in which Great Britain through the years has always played the

leading _____.

2. Letters for numbers

A = 2   B = 4   C = 12 D = 8   E = 20

What are the answers to the following sums? Write your answer as a letter.

a.   C - A = _____ ÷ 2

b.   E - _____ = D x 2

c.   A x B = E - _____

d.   E x B = _____ x 10

3.   Letter connections

A B C D E F G H I J K L M N O P Q R S T U V W X Y Z

Find the pair of letters that will complete the sentence in the most sensible way.

Example   AE is to CG as IM is to KO

a.   ZA is to ON as QP is to   _____

b.   PR is to LJ as TV is to   _____

c.   XS is to YZ as KF is to   _____

d.   HO is to FD as TA is to   _____

Test 20

1. Complete the sum

For each question find the missing number that will complete the sum and write it in the space provided.

a. $17 \times 3 = 34 + \underline{\hspace{1.5cm}}$

b. $100 \div (4 \times 5) = 5 \times \underline{\hspace{1.5cm}}$

c. $(18 \div 6) \times 3 = 90 \div \underline{\hspace{1.5cm}}$

d. $(125 \div 5) \times 3 = 100 - \underline{\hspace{1.5cm}}$

2. Make a word

The three words in the second group must go together in the same way as the three words in the first group. Find the missing word and write it in the space provided.

Example   (man [mat] tip)   (bug [**bud**] dew)

'mat' is formed by using the first two letters of 'man' and the first of 'tip', therefore the missing word uses the first two letters of 'bug' and the first of 'dew'

a.   (search [near] lotion)   (camera [_____] strong)

b.   (sin [sit] lit)   (par [_____] day)

c.   (peanut [teal] brazil)   (coward [_____] brawn)

d.   (float [leaf] taper)   (dream [_____] label)

43

3. Number series

Complete the missing numbers in the following sequences.

Example	2	4	6	8	<u>10</u>	<u>12</u>

a.	97	86	96	85	95	84	___
b.	200	40	50	10	20	4	___
c.	2	3	5	7	11	13	___
d.	1	4	9	16	25	36	___

Test 21

1. Same meaning

One word, from the options given, will go equally well with both sets of words in brackets. Underline the correct word as shown in the example.

Example   (globe, planet)   (soil, mud)

    Options: (<u>earth</u>, brown, ground, pluto, circle)

a.   (turned, coil)   (damage, harm)

    Options: (split, folded, wound, corner, tribute)

b.   (rip, gash)   (cry, weep)

    Options: (heal, tear, walk, rebel, walk)

c.   (rubbish, waste)   (deny, reject)

    Options: (refuse, withdraw, garbage, accept, inflate)

d.   (fair, just)   (correct, true)

    Options: (faithful, value, right, rough, strong)

2. Make a word

The three words in the second group must go together in the same way as the three words in the first group. Find the missing word and write it in the space provided.

Example   (man [mat] tip)   (bug [**bud**] dew)

a.   (elite [tide] spade)   (alone [_____] chase)

b.   (idea [epic] crop)   (last [_____] demo)

c.   (grape [trap] table)   (stone [_____] sunny)

d.   (arise [rage] gears)   (paste [_____] moans)

3. Two odd ones out

Three of the words in the list are linked in some way. Mark the words that are not linked, as shown in the example :

Example :   ~~dog~~   crow   ~~cat~~   magpie   eagle

1.   banana   apple   almond   plum   hazelnut

2.   listen   swim   walk   run   smell

3.   metal   hammer   screwdriver   wood   pliers

4.   flea   fly   beetle   rat   mouse

5.   bake   peel   fry   roast   core

Test 22

1. Letter connections

A B C D E F G H I J K L M N O P Q R S T U V W X Y Z

Find the pair of letters that will complete the sentence in the most sensible way.

Example   AE is to CG as IM is to KO

a.   ET is to VG as BV is to   _____

b.   FJ is to CP as QU is to   _____

c.   BJ is to PQ as LS is to   _____

d.   LK is to FQ as SR is to   _____

2. Word connections

Find two words, one from each group, that will complete the sentence in the most sensible way. Underline the two words.

Example   Big is to (small, orange, colour) as wide is to (apple, red, narrow).

a.   Shoe is to (head, arm, foot) as glove is to (leg, arm, hand).

b.   Pup is to (owl, seal, lion) as foal is to (fox, dog, horse).

c.   Near is to (close, far, distant) as high is to (low, climb, jump).

d.   Driver is to (bicycle, ship, bus) as helmsman is to (car, boat, plane)

3.   Related numbers

Look at the relationship between the first and last number in each set of brackets and use that relationship to find the missing number.

Example   (16 [4] 4)   (15 [3] 5)   (12 [4] 3)

a.   (6 [24] 12)   (15 [40] 10)   (14 [?] 8)

b.   (2 [18] 18)   (6 [18] 6)   (3 [?] 10)

c.   (10 [21] 10)   (3 [8] 4)   (23 [?] 18)

d.   (7 [4] 28)   (9 [3] 27)   (8 [?] 32)

Test 23

1. Reading information

Five birds are perched on branches in the same tree. A wren is perched two branches lower than a raven but one branch higher than a robin. A blackbird is sitting on the branch above the wren. A magpie is singing from the branch below the raven.

a.   Which two birds are perched on the same branch? _____

b.   Which bird is on the lowest branch?   _____

2. Word and number codes

You are given four words and three codes. The words and codes are in no particular order. Three of the codes match three of the words, one word has no code. Can you answer the following questions?

PART   TRIP   CARS   CAST

1257   6287   7896

a.   What is the code for STAIR?   _____

b.   What does 62895 mean?   _____

c.   What is the code for STRICT?   _____

3. Related words

A B C D E F G H I J K L M N O P Q R S T U V W X Y Z

a. If the code for WASH is RWPF,
   what is the code for SOAP? _____ NKXN

b. If the code for SECOND is XORIMH,
   what is the code for FOURTH? _____ KYJLSL

c. If the code for BLACK is CMBDL,
   what is the code for WHITE? _____ XIJUF

d. If the code for GOAT is EMYR,
   what does DPME mean? _____ FROG

Did you know goats are extremely useful animals. Apart from the fact that their meat is eaten worldwide, they also provide us with leather and milk.
Goat's milk can be turned into butter, cheese and yoghurt, just like cow's milk.

Test 24

1. Same meaning

One word, from the options given, will go equally well with both sets of words in brackets. Underline the correct word.

Example   (globe, planet)   (soil, mud)

      Options   (earth, brown, ground, pluto, circle)

a.   (coins, money)   (alter, amend)

     Options: (repair, trial, review, change, passage)

b.   (adjacent, near)   (shut, lock)

     Options: (beneath, through, along, close, begin)

c.   (cover, screen)   (colour, hue)

     Options: (grime, shine, place, shade, wealth)

d.   (second, hour)   (small, tiny)

     Options: (regal, whole, timed, minute, little)

2. Word and number codes

You are given four words and three codes. The words and codes are in no particular order. Three of the codes match three of the words, one word has no code. Can you answer the following questions?

KITE   POET   INTO   PAIN

5716   8457   3512

a.   What is the code for KITE?   _____

b.   What does 8243 mean?   _____

c.   What is the code for KNOT?   _____

3. Related words

A B C D E F G H I J K L M N O P Q R S T U V W X Y Z

The alphabet has been provided to help you. Can you crack the codes and answer the following questions?

a.   If the code for WALK is XCOO,
        what is the code for RIDE?   _____

b.   If the code for GRASS is IPCQU,
        what is the code for BUNCH?   _____

c.   If the code for QUILT is RWLPY,
        what is the code for COVER?   _____

Test 25

1. Word connections

Find two words, one from each group, that will complete the sentence in the most sensible way. Underline the two words.

Example   Big is to (<u>small</u>, orange, colour) as wide is to (apple, red, <u>narrow</u>).

a.   Hoof is to (dog, horse, weasel) as paw is to (cat, goat, sheep).

b.   Pig is to (mutton, veal, pork) as cow is to (lamb, beef, venison).

c.   Shout is to (whisper, loud, follow) as bold is to (banter, timid, brave).

d.   Hole is to (entire, whole, dig) as grown is to (groan, whistle, full)

2. Complete the sum

For each question find the missing number that will complete the sum and write it in the space provided.

a. $4^2 \div 8 = 100 \div$ _____

b. $14 \div$ _____ $= 102 \div 51$

c. $(5 \times 3) \times 3 = 32 +$ _____ $+ 5$

d.   _____ $\div 6 = 24 - 6 \div 3$

3.   Reading information

Read the following two statements then underline the option below which must be true based solely on the information in the two statements.
.
French and Spanish are languages. France and Spain are in Europe.

a.   French and Spanish are widely spoken languages.

b.   Germans are Europeans.

c.   People in Spain are bilingual.

d.   French is a European language.

Did you know, the word for someone who can speak two different languages is 'bilingual', the word for someone who can speak three languages is 'trilingual', fluency in four languages makes you 'quadrilingual' and five languages makes you 'pentalingual'. The term for someone who speaks many languages is 'polyglot'.
That's five new words for your word bank. Why not find out what they are in another language!

Test 26

1. Letters for numbers

$A = 9$ $B = 2$ $C = 27$ $D = 3$ $E = 81$

What are the answers to the following sums? Write your answer as a letter.

a. $(C \div D) \times A =$ _____

b. $E \div$ _____ $= 3 \times A$

c. $ABD =$ _____ $- C$

d. $10 \times D - B =$ _____ $+ 1$

2. Word connections

Find two words, one from each group, that will complete the sentence in the most sensible way. Underline the two words.

Example   Big is to (<u>small</u>, orange, colour) as wide is to (apple, red, <u>narrow</u>).

a.   Blue is to (sun, cloud, sky) as green is to (flower, petal, grass).

b.   Femur is to (shoulder, leg, foot) as ulna is to (neck, knee, arm).

c.   Trowel is to (reading, driving, gardening) as polish is to (ironing, dusting, cooking).

d.   Lie is to (bed, floor, falsehood) as honest is to (stand, recline, frank).

3.   Compound words

Can you find a word that can be put after each of the following words to create a new compound word.

Example   door   rail   alley   passage   **way**

a.   copy   under   type   screen   _____

b.   brother   child   widow   sister   _____

c.   flag   space   lord   star   _____

d.   blind   river   ring   bed   _____

Did you know Qamdo Bamda Airport in China has the world's longest runway at a mighty 5500m. By contrast, Juancho E Yrausquin Airport on the Dutch Caribbean island of Saba has the world's shortest runway at a miniscule 399m!

Test 27

1. Complete the word

Find the word that completes the third pair of words in the same way as the first two pairs of words.

a.   (HINDER, RIND)   (RENTED, DENT)   (PARTED,   _____)

b.   (WANTED, WADE)   (LOITER, LORE)   (DUFFLE,   _____)

c.   (FLOOD, GOOD)   (BOAST, CAST)   (STALE,   _____)

d.   (RENT, TORE)   (VEAL, LOVE)   (TEAR,   _____)

2. Letter series

Complete the missing pairs of letters in the following sequences.
The alphabet has been given to help you.

A B C D E F G H I J K L M N O P Q R S T U V W X Y Z

Example	FS	IQ	HO	**KM**	JK	**MI**

a.   AC   DF   GI   JL   _____   _____

b.   ZW   _____   YV   YZ   XU   _____

c.   ST   _____   SV   SW   _____   SY

d.   FD   GE   HF   IG   _____   _____

3.   Hidden words

Can you find a four letter word hidden in each of the following sentences. The word will consist of a letter or letters from the end of one word and a letter or letters from the start of the next word.

Example   I used yours after mine ran out.   **term** (af**ter m**ine)

a.   The blanket was laid over the bed.   _____

b   The tarmac was laid on the road.   _____

c.   Jane hates talking in front of people.   _____

d.   Emma set the oven too high.   _____

Did you know 'tarmac' is short for 'tarmacadam'. Macadam roads were pioneered by Scottish engineer John Loudon McAdam in the 1820's. They consisted of pressed stones and stone dust. With the advent of motor vehicles around 100 years later there was a need to strengthen the roads and tar was used to bind the stones and stone dust together to create a smoother surface and to reduce the clouds of dust created by the vehicles.

Test 28

1. Same meaning

One word, from the options given, will go equally well with both sets of words in brackets. Underline the correct word.

     Example   (globe, planet)   (soil, mud)

          Options: (earth, brown, ground, pluto, circle)

a.   (pure, spotless)   (improve, refine)

    Options: (faulty, intact, revolve, taste, perfect)

b.   (crop, harvest)   (make, generate)

    Options: (cut, form, valid, reduce, produce)

c.   (empty, seep)   (pipe, sewer)

    Options: (gutter, drain, delete, flow, wither)

d.   (location, site)   (put, seat)

    Options: (house, reside, place, map, chair)

2. Complete the word

Find the word that completes the third pair of words in the same way as the first two pairs of words.

a.   (RISK, WHISK)   (ROSE, WHOSE)   (RAM,   )

b.   (STRAW, WARTS)   (STAR, RATS)   (DEVIL,   )

c.   (CUSTARD, CARD)   (VIOLENT, VENT)   (SAILING,   )

d.   (RETIRE, RITE)   (SPARES, ERAS)   (DECIDE,   )

3. Letter connections

A B C D E F G H I J K L M N O P Q R S T U V W X Y Z

Find the pair of letters that will complete the sentences in the most sensible way.

Example   AE is to CG as IM is to KO

a.   AZB is to BYC as CXD is to _____

b.   PLW is to RNU as FJK is to _____

c.   NM is to QP as TS is to _____

d.   GIG is to IKI as KMK is to _____

Test 29

1. Reading information

Mary, Jack and Emma left school at 3.30pm. Mary arrived home first. Jack arrived home five minutes later than Mary, at 3.50pm. Emma arrived home last, 25 minutes after Mary.

a.   What time did Mary arrive home?   _____

b.   How many minutes later than Jack did Emma arrive home?   _____

2. Related numbers

Look at the relationship between the first and last number in each set of brackets and use that relationship to find the missing number.

Example	(16 [4] 4)	(15 [3] 5)	(12 [4] 3)
a.	(1 [4] 9)	(16 [25] 36)	(49 [?] 81)
b.	(2 [18] 3)	(4 [60] 5)	(3 [?] 9)
c.	(21 [8] 11)	(16 [5] 4)	(24 [?] 4)
d.	(14 [18] 11)	(8 [23] 19)	(12 [?] 11)

3. Make a word

The three words in the second group must go together in the same way as the three words in the first group. Find the missing word and write it in the space provided.

Example   (man [mat] tip)   (bug [**bud**] dew)

'mat' is formed by using the first two letters of 'man' and the first of 'tip', therefore the missing word uses the first two letters of 'bug' and the first of 'dew'

a.   (grand [art] dealt)   (barge [__ear__] clear)

b.   (taught [tent] design)   (reacts [__star__] stigma)

c.   (cream [liar] lived)   (snail [__rain__] rapid)

d.   (alive [pole] group)   (opens [__tops__] ghost)

Did you know, barges are flat-bottomed boats built mainly to transport goods along rivers and canals. Originally they would have been pulled by horses that walked along a towpath at the side of the waterway but nowadays barges are either self-propelled or pulled by tugboats.

Test 30

1.   Number series

Complete the missing numbers in the following sequences.

Example   2   4   6   8   <u>10</u>   <u>12</u>

a.   8   24   40   56   72   88   _____

b.   79   _____   65   58   51   _____   37

c.   80   41   71   _____   62   23   _____

d.   34   41   43   50   _____   59   _____

2.   Missing word

Find the three letter word that is missing from the capitalised letters to form a new word.
Write the three letter word and the complete new word as shown in the example.

Example   Tom will GLY do it for you.   <u>LAD, GLADLY</u>

a.   VEGELES are full of vitamins and minerals.   _____

b.   Tom took his LUGE from the conveyor belt.   _____

c.   Elijah got a FASTIC score in his test.   _____

d.   Simon decided to attend a COLE in Oxford.   _____

e.   The car SDED on the icy road.   _____

3.   Related words

A B C D E F G H I J K L M N O P Q R S T U V W X Y Z

The alphabet has been provided to help you.
Can you crack the codes and answer the following questions?

a.   If the code for NUMBER is QSPZHP,
          what is the code for ABACUS?   _____

b.   If the code for FLINT is ENFRO,
          what does RVLRZ mean?   _____

c.   If the code for GAME is HCNG,
          what is the code for DICE?   _____

Answers

Test 1

1. Opposite meaning

a. resist, accede
b. heed, disregard
c. flourish, wither
d. neaten, disorganise
e. excavate, bury

2. Closest in meaning

a. shrink, contract
b. purposeful, deliberate
c. confused, bewildered
d. hurt, wound

3. Choose a word

1. boom
2. journal
3. cartography
4. flourishing
5. risen
6. base

Test 2

1. Fill in the missing words

The Yorkshire Rebellion was **sparked** off by resentment of the taxation granted by Parliament in 1489 in **order** to finance the involvement of English forces in the campaign in Brittany, France. It became particularly **notorious** because of the murder, by the rebels, of the Earl of Northumberland just **outside** Topcliffe near Thirsk in the North Riding of Yorkshire in April of that year. There are not many **details** surrounding the rebellion but the Earl of Northumberland was considered to be a victim of resentment against taxation.

2.   Closest in meaning

a.   assessment, evaluation
b.   reject, decline
c.   petty, trivial
d.   inferior, worse

3.   Idioms

A blessing in disguise	c	a. good luck
Cut someone some slack	e	b. get out of control
Break a leg	a	c. a good thing that seemed bad at first
Get out of hand	b	d. don't give up
Hang in there	d	e. don't be so critical

4.   Opposite meaning

a.   educated, ignorant
b.   famous, unknown
c.   plural, singular
d.   reality, fantasy
e.   inaudible, loud

Test 3

1.   Opposite meaning

a.   scarce, plentiful
b.   vague, precise
c.   include, omit
d.   supporter, traitor
e.   perilous, safe

2. Fill in the missing words

The use of sliding parts in furniture gave us the **extending** or draw leaf dining table. First **introduced** during the late sixteenth **century**, this type of table became popular in the Jacobean period. Variations of the draw leaf construction were produced throughout the **ensuing** periods to the present day, and many of our modern extending tables work on the same basic principle as the Elizabethan version. When closed, the table looks like a long **dining** table with legs.

3. Word Groups

salmon	D
elm	C
oak	C
flu	A
orange	B
eel	D
fever	A
beech	C
lemon	B
plaice	D

Test 4

1. Opposite meaning

a. increase, reduce
b. calm, turbulent
c. elementary, complicated
d. generous, miserly
e. halt, continue

2. Insert a letter

bor (**e**) ast   boo (**k**) nee   gro (**w**) ish   tea (**t**) ick

crow (**n**) od   pon (**d**) uck   sit (**e**) ver   pos (**t**) uck

3. Idioms

Miss the boat	b	a. To stop doing something
To get bent out of shape	d	b. It's too late
Call it a day	a	c. To be treated as you treat others (usually badly)
By the skin of your teeth	e	d. To get upset about something
Get a taste of your own medicine	c	e. Just barely

Test 5

1. Opposite meaning

a. fruitful, futile
b. inflexible, bendy
c. dusk, dawn
d. special, ordinary
e. lazy, energetic

2. Hidden words

a. Here
b. omen
c. rope
d. pope
e. draw

3. Alphabetical order

FLOWERS   O
PROTEIN   O
HIGHEST   H
WEBSITE   I

4. Insert two letters

a. dy
b. al
c. el
d. ad
e. ce

Test 6

1. Number series

a. 26
b. 45
c. 49
d. 63

2. Missing word

a. EAR, BEARD
b. OUR, JOURNEY
c SIN, RAISINS
d. TOO, STOOD
e. HAM, HAMMER

3. Move a letter

a. water   brain
b. riven   draft
c. fend   pain
d. clan   cape
e. lame   falter

4. Opposite meaning

a. friend, foe
b. tranquil, agitated
c. respectful, impudent
d. continue, abandon

Test 7

1.   **Alphabetical order**

a.   ACILMNOP
b.   N
c.   FAINT FIGHT FLAT FLIGHT FLOAT

2.   **Compound words**

a.   man
b.   fly
c.   bridge
d.   fish

3.   **Closest in meaning**

a.   luminous, bright
b.   remain, linger
c.   peckish, hungry
d.   stack, heap
e.   elude, avoid

Test 8

1.   **Change one word**

a.	lazy	changes to	**fit**
b.	shut	changes to	**opened**
c.	hungry	changes to	**thirsty**
d.	easy	changes to	**hard**

2.   **Fill in the missing words**

There is no **act** of Parliament forbidding the pasturing of bulls in fields crossed by public paths, but most counties have a **byelaw** which makes it illegal to have a bull more than twelve months old in a field containing a public path. Some counties allow bulls in fields with paths provided that cows are **present**, on the grounds that the bull will be more interested in the cows than in walkers. It is **illegal** to have any animal known to be dangerous in a field crossed by a public path and the owner is **liable** for any damage or injury that the beast may cause.

3. Two odd ones out

a.	~~banana~~	parsnip	carrot	~~apple~~	turnip
b.	~~glass~~	ocean	lake	~~water~~	pond
c.	cherish	love	~~detest~~	adore	~~abhor~~
d.	~~fox~~	lion	~~frog~~	jaguar	cheetah
e.	~~subside~~	ascend	rise	~~descend~~	mount

Test 9

1. Number series

a. 23
b. 73
c. 19
d. 79

2. Closest in meaning

a. turbulent, tempestuous
b. cremate, incinerate
c. flawless, perfect
d. extricate, release
e. damp, moist

3. Alphabetical order

a. SPLOTCH
b. SPEARED
c. SPECKLE
d. SPIRIT

Test 10

1. Compound words

a. ever
b. port
c. yard
d. print

2.   Fill in the missing words

Minerals are **chemical** substances that occur naturally in the **crust** of the earth. Rocks are **masses** of one or more minerals. Three great classes of rocks are distinguished: igneous (those that solidified from the **molten** state); sedimentary (those formed as a result of the erosion of pre-existing rocks and the redeposition of the resulting material); and metamorphic (rocks formed by the effects of **pressure** and/or heat on existing rocks).

3.   Insert two letters

a.   st
b.   ed
c.   al
d.   ce
e.   ic

Test 11

1.   Letter series

a.   EL
b.   VE
c.   UV (the vowels in alphabetical order, followed by the next letter)
d.   MK

2.   Opposite meaning

a.   smile, frown
b.   active, docile
c.   ally, foe
d.   base, apex
e.   nadir, top

3.   Missing word

a.   HER, GATHERED
b.   LIE, BELIEVABLE
c.   OLD, HOUSEHOLD
d.   LET, MISTLETOE
e.   RUE, INCONGRUENT

Test 12

1.   Move a letter

a.   bacon   event
b.   sting   cramp
c.   moves   hoist
d.   pith   hatch

2.   Fill in the missing words

The Thames rises in the **foothills** of the Cotswolds and flows eastwards towards Oxford, searching, it seems, for a gap in the chalk hills to the south. At Oxford it turns south having **found** the gap between the Berkshire Downs and the Chilterns. At this **stage** it has grown so wide it appears almost to fill the gap and to leave no room for those twin villages of Streatley and Goring. At Reading, with the help of the river Kennet, it decides to **investigate** the slopes of the Chilterns. At Marlow the river becomes bored with the chalk and flows southeast through Eton and Windsor, but at Weybridge it is the sea that urges it to flow eastward again through London, and on to lose itself beyond the **estuary**.

3.   Change one word

a.   lost   changes to   **won**
b.   sounded   changes to   **looked**
c.   lock   changes to   **keys (or key)**
d.   yesterday   changes to   **today**

Test 13

1.   Insert a letter

a.   g
b.   h
c.   e
d.   y
e.   n

2.   Word Groups

happiness	A
window	D
lobster	C
floor	D
taupe	B
shrimp	C
sorrow	A
ceiling	D
regret	A
lilac	B

3.   Hidden words

a.   seam
b.   door
c.   gene
d.   real or slat
e.   reap

Test 14

1.   Word swaps

a.   David wrote a long <u>letter</u> before putting it in the envelope ready to <u>post</u>.
b.   Susan <u>wore</u> her <u>new</u> hat.
c.   Peter took <u>swimming</u> lessons on Tuesday <u>evening</u>.
d.   Always <u>remember</u> to <u>look</u> before crossing the road.
e.   I hope I <u>will</u> do <u>well</u> this afternoon.

2.   Opposite meaning

a.   destroy, build
b.   perfect, faulty
c.   comic, tragic
d.   artificial, genuine
e.   unlucky, fortunate

3. Move a letter

a.	badge	frog
b.	sea	ledge
c.	tap	front
d.	pus	bath
e.	ash	burn

Test 15

1. Number series

a. 64, 128
b. 31, 50
c. 9, 9
d. 9, 14
e. 46, 82

2. Letter series

a. OL, QN
b. UH, TI
c. ZA, QJ
d. MQ, QQ

3. Related words

a. VKPA
b. UTNAMD
c. KGZIQ
d. XEHEJGA

Test 16

1. Related numbers

a.	66	*1st number + 3rd number = 2nd number*
b.	71	*1st number - 2nd number = 3rd number*
c.	18	*1st number x 3rd number = 2nd number*
d.	3	*2nd number x 3rd number = 1st number*

2.   Alphabetical order

a.   boulder
b.   crispy
c.   water
d.   foreign

3.   Letters for numbers

a.   B
b.   E
c.   E
d.   A

Test 17

1.   Opposite meaning

a.   pompous, humble
b.   radical, conservative
c.   motley, uniform
d.   raw, cooked

2.   Two odd ones out

a.	femur	ulna	radius	~~bicep~~	~~deltoid~~
b.	~~circle~~	square	~~triangle~~	rhombus	trapezoid
c.	paper	blackboard	~~pen~~	whiteboard	~~pencil~~
d.	beef	pork	~~pig~~	~~cow~~	venison
e.	France	Germany	~~Mexico~~	~~Texas~~	Spain

3.   Missing words

1. has
2. that
3. into
4. an
5. who

Test 18

1.   Complete the sum

a.   4
b.   2
c.   10
d.   80

2.   Closest in meaning

a.   evil, wicked
b.   broad, wide
c.   terrified, horrified
d.   harsh, cruel
e.   brief, short

3.   Two odd ones out

a.	red	green	~~flag~~	~~pole~~	blue
b.	guitar	~~music~~	~~volume~~	violin	cello
c.	see	hear	~~sound~~	smell	~~nose~~
d.	snow	sleet	~~sun~~	rain	~~rays~~
e.	~~shirt~~	trilby	~~moccasins~~	bowler	cap

Test 19

1.   Fill in the missing words

The spirit of cycling is very much alive in most of **the** countries of the world, and it looks as though it will continue that way for a long time to come, certainly as long as there are **active** people wishing to travel about in the most convenient and inexpensive way imaginable. It would be almost impossible to **compute** the number of bicycles in existence—certainly several millions in this **country** alone, and this represents a major industry in which Great Britain through the years has always played the leading **part**.

2.   Letters for numbers

a.   E
b.   B
c.   C
d.   D

3.   Letter connections

a.   FE
b.   PN
c.   LM
d.   RP

Test 20

1.   Complete the sum

a.   17
b.   1
c.   10
d.   25

2.   Make a word

a.   game
b.   pay
c.   down
d.   read

3.   Number series

a.   94
b.   14
c.   17
d.   49

Test 21

1.   Same meaning

a.   wound
b.   tear
c.   refuse
d.   right

2. Make a word

a. nose
b. sold
c. stun
d. name

3. Two odd ones out

1.	banana	apple	~~almond~~	plum	~~hazelnut~~
2.	~~listen~~	swim	walk	run	~~smell~~
3.	~~metal~~	hammer	screwdriver	~~wood~~	pliers
4.	flea	fly	beetle	~~rat~~	~~mouse~~
5.	bake	~~peel~~	fry	roast	~~core~~

Test 22

1. Letter connections

a. SI
b. NA
c. ZZ
d. MX

2. Word connections

a. foot, hand
b. seal, horse
c. far, low
d. bus, boat

3. Related numbers

a. 36   *(2nd number - 3rd number) ÷ 2 = 1st number*
b. 15   *(2nd number ÷ 1st number) x 2= 3rd number*
c. 42   *1st number + 3rd number + 1 = 2nd number*
d. 4   *3rd number ÷ 1st number = 2nd number*

Test 23

1.   Reading information

a.   blackbird, magpie
b.   robin

2.   Word and number codes

a.   57298
b.   PARIS
c.   578917

3.   Related words

a.   NKXN
b.   KYJLSL
c.   FROG

Test 24

1.   Same meaning

a.   change
b.   close
c.   shade
d.   minute

2.   Word and number codes

a.   3512
b.   PEAK
c.   3761

3.   Related words

a.   SKGI
b.   DSPAJ
c.   DQYIW

Test 25

1. Word connections

a. horse, cat
b. pork, beef
c. whisper, timid
d. whole, groan

2. Complete the sum

a. 50
b. 2
c. 8
d. 36

3. Reading information

d. French is a European language.

Test 26

1. Letters for numbers

a. E
b. D
c. E
d. C

2. Word connections

a. sky, grass
b. leg, arm
c. gardening, dusting
d. falsehood, frank

3.   Compound words

a.   writer
b.   hood
c.   ship
d.   side

Test 27

1.   Complete the word

a.   DART
b.   DUEL
c.   TALE
d.   ROTE

2.   Letter series

a.   MO, PR
b.   ZA, XY
c.   SU, SX
d.   JH, KI

3.   Hidden words
a.   dove
b.   hero
c.   test
d.   vent or sett

Test 28

1.   Same meaning

a.   perfect
b.   produce
c.   drain
d.   place

2.   Complete the word

a.   WHAM
b.   LIVED
c.   SING
d.   DICE

3.   Letter connections

a.   DWE
b.   HLI
c.   WV
d.   MOM

Test 29

1.   Reading information

a.   3.45pm
b.   20 minutes

2.   Related numbers

a.   64   *1 x 1 = 1st number, 2 x 2 = 2nd number...8 x 8 = 8th number*
b.   81   *(1st number x 3rd number) x 3 = 2nd number*
c.   7   *(1st number + 3rd number) ÷ 4 = 2nd number*
d.   17   *(1st number ÷ 2) + 3rd number = 2nd number*

3.   Make a word

a.   ear
b.   star
c.   rain
d.   tops

Test 30

1.   Number series

a.   104
b.   72, 44
c.   32, 53
d.   52, 61

2.   Missing word

a.   TAB, VEGETABLES
b.   GAG, LUGGAGE
c.   ANT, FANTASTIC
d.   LEG, COLLEGE
e.   KID, SKIDDED

3.   Related words
a.   DZDAXQ
b.   STONE
c.   EKDG

Printed in Great Britain
by Amazon

57765542R00050